ENDANGERED ANIMALS

Endangered Animals on the GRASSLANDS

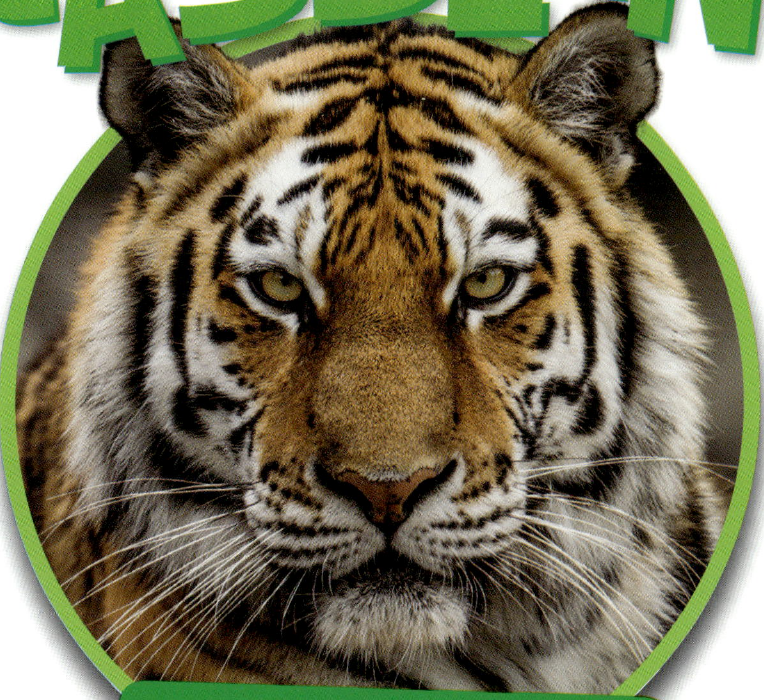

By Emilie Dufresne

PowerKiDS press™

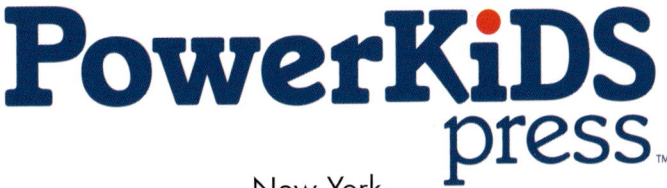

New York

Published in 2022 by The Rosen Publishing Group, Inc.
29 East 21st Street, New York, NY 10010

© 2022 Booklife Publishing
This edition is published by arrangement with Booklife Publishing

Written by:
Emilie Dufresne

Edited by:
Madeline Tyler

Designed by:
Jasmine Pointer

Cataloging-in-Publication Data
Names: Dufresne, Emilie.
Title: Endangered animals on the grasslands / Emilie Dufresne.
Description: New York : PowerKids Press, 2022. | Series: Endangered animals | Includes glossary and index.
Identifiers: ISBN 9781725336346 (pbk.) | ISBN 9781725336360 (library bound) | ISBN 9781725336353 (6 pack) | ISBN 9781725336377 (ebook)
Subjects: LCSH: Grassland animals--Juvenile literature. | Grassland animals--Conservation--Juvenile literature. | Endangered species--Juvenile literature.
Classification: LCC QL115.3 D84 2022 | DDC 591.74--dc23

All rights reserved. No part of this book may be reproduced in any form without permission in writing from the publisher, except by a reviewer.

Manufactured in the United States of America

CPSIA Compliance Information: Batch #CWPK22. For Further Information contact Rosen Publishing, New York, New York at 1-800-237-9932.

Find us on

PHOTO CREDITS

All images are courtesy of Shutterstock.com, unless otherwise specified. With thanks to Getty Images, Thinkstock Photo and iStockphoto. Cover – Henner Damke, Maciej Czekajewski. 4–5 – Positive Snapshot, Konoplytska, CarolinDr. 6–7 – leolintang. 8–9 – Veranika848, osap, alicja neumiler. 10–11 – Dirk M. de Boer, Cathy Withers-Clarke, Zhenyakot, Emma Geary. 12–13 – hallam creations, Kikinusska, chonlasub woravichan, Fabian Plock. 14–15 – Denise Allison Coyle, Sourabh Bharti. 16–17 – EcoPrint, Lucian Coman, Igillustrator. 18–19 – R. Maximiliane, silverfox999, Simon Dannhauer, VOLYK IEVGENII. 20–21 – Lothar Schlawe / Public domain, Wuttichok Panichiwarapun, APIWICH PUDSUMRAN, Byron Layton. 22–23 – Thorsten Spoerlein, Piotr Swat, HelloRF Zcool, Photographee.eu.

CONTENTS

Page 4   Being Endangered
Page 6   A Closer Look at the Categories
Page 8   The Grassland Habitat
Page 10 Black Rhinoceroses
Page 12 Pygmy Hippopotamuses
Page 14 Tigers
Page 16 African Elephants
Page 18 Hooded Vultures
Page 20 Now Extinct
Page 21 Success Stories
Page 22 Save the Animals!
Page 24 Glossary and Index

Words that look like <u>this</u> can be found in the glossary on page 24.

Being ENDANGERED

When a <u>species</u> of animal is endangered, it means that it is in danger of going extinct. When a species is extinct, it means there are no more of that animal left alive in the world.

Pangolins are an endangered animal.

There are many different reasons that a species might become endangered. If a species' habitat is changed or polluted, the species could become endangered.

Many grassland animals are losing their habitats because of farming.

5

A Closer Look at the CATEGORIES

Different species are put into different categories depending on how <u>threatened</u> they are.

Data Deficient — Not enough information to know what category the species is in

Least Concern — Currently not in danger of going extinct

Near Threatened — Likely to be threatened soon

Vulnerable — Facing a high <u>risk</u> of extinction in the wild

Always check this website to find the most up-to-date information...

www.iucnredlist.org

Endangered — Facing a very high risk of extinction in the wild

Critically Endangered — Facing extremely high risk of extinction in the wild

Extinct in the Wild — When a species can no longer be found in the wild and only lives in <u>captivity</u>

Extinct — When a species no longer exists in the world

The GRASSLAND HABITAT

Grasslands get more rain than deserts but less rain than forests. Most of the plants on grasslands are grasses. There are also a few trees.

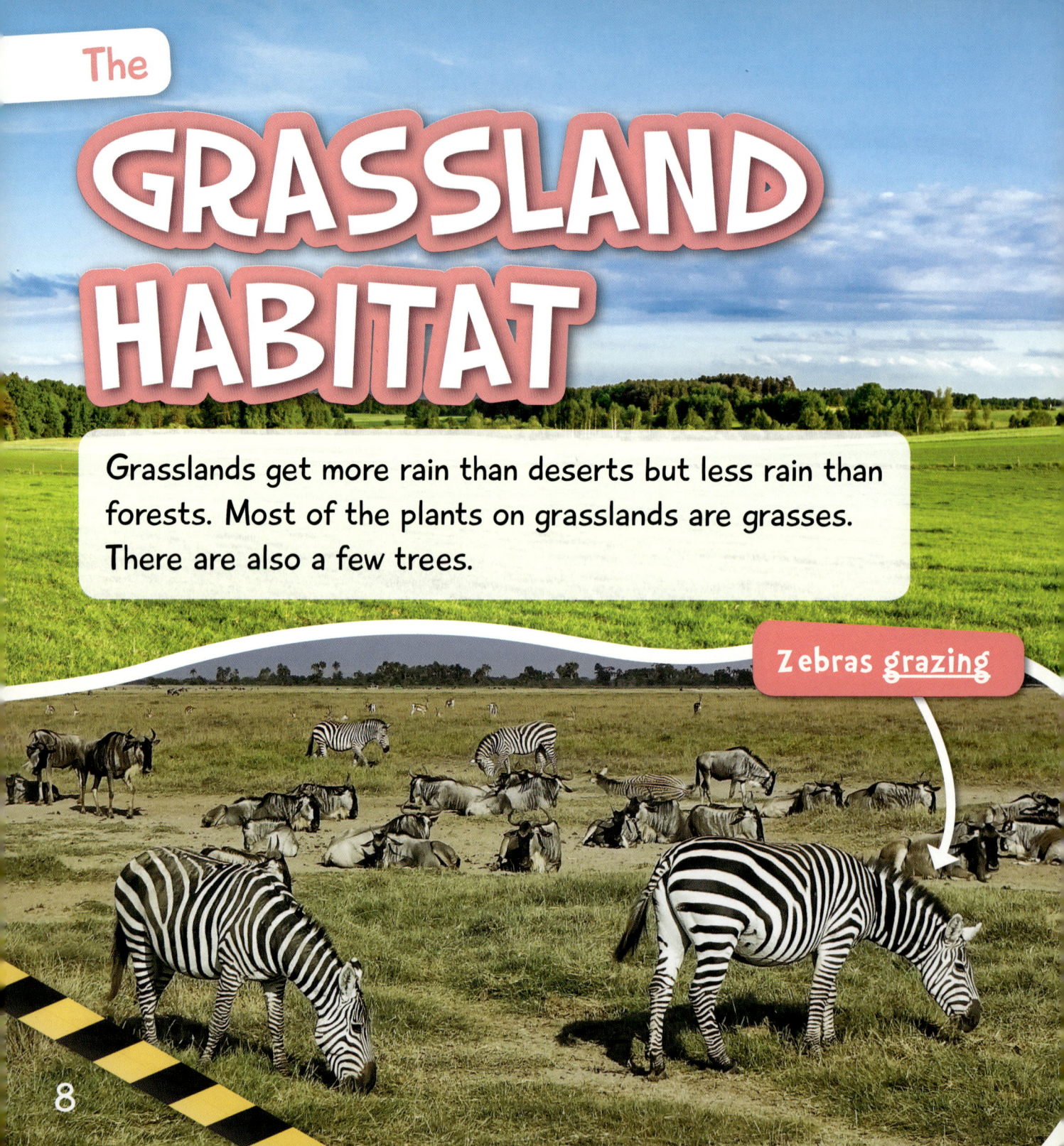

Zebras grazing

There are different grassland habitats all over the world. Humans create many problems for grassland animals because they use their habitat for building or farming.

These deer have had a city built on their habitat.

Black RHINOCEROSES

Poaching is the biggest threat black rhinoceroses face. They are hunted for their horns, which are sold illegally.

NAME:
Black rhinoceros

FOUND:
Southern Africa

CATEGORY:
Critically endangered

POPULATION:
Around 3,000

Black rhinoceroses are <u>protected</u> from poachers and their population is increasing in some places. It is still important to make sure they are protected.

You can help protect rhinos by visiting this website:
savetherhino.org

• Black rhinoceroses found

Pygmy HIPPOPOTAMUSES

Pygmy hippopotamuses are threatened by farming. Their habitat is being used to produce coffee, rubber, and palm oil.

Pygmy hippopotamuses found

Pygmy hippopotamuses are forced to move towards human habitats as they lose more of their land. This means they are more likely to be hunted and killed.

Pygmy hippopotamuses also live in forests, rivers, and lakes as well as grasslands.

NAME:
Pygmy hippopotamus

FOUND:
Small areas in West Africa

CATEGORY:
Endangered

POPULATION:
Over 2,000

13

TIGERS

Tigers are illegally hunted for their skin, bones, and meat. Many tigers have been pushed out of their habitats into places they are not used to.

NAME:
Tiger

FOUND:
Across southern Asia and eastern Asia

CATEGORY:
Endangered

POPULATION:
Between 2,000 and 3,000

Tigers are also losing large areas of their habitat. Their habitat is being used for farming and to make space for people to live.

Tigers found

Tigers are forced to leave protected areas to find food.

African ELEPHANTS

Poaching is the biggest threat to African elephants. They are hunted for their meat and tusks. Their tusks are made of ivory, which is illegally bought and sold.

African elephants can be hurt by people who are scared of the damage the elephants may cause.

African elephants found

NAME:
African elephant

FOUND:
Across Africa

CATEGORY:
Vulnerable

African elephants crossing a road

Elephants are losing their habitat because of farming and building. They are being forced into areas with more people in them.

17

Hooded VULTURES

Hooded vultures are hunted for their meat. They are also used to make medicine in some areas.

• Hooded vultures found

Medicine is used to try to make people feel better when they are ill.

Hooded vultures find dead animals and eat whatever may be left of them. Some poachers poison hooded vultures so they don't give away where the poachers have illegally killed other animals.

NAME:
Hooded vulture

FOUND:
Across Africa

CATEGORY:
Critically endangered

Poisoning is when someone adds something to food that can harm or kill another animal.

Now
EXTINCT

Schomburgk's deer went extinct in the 1930s. It used to live on the grasslands of Thailand but it lost almost all of its habitat to rice farming.

Antlers of Schomburgk's deer

SUCCESS STORIES

The bald eagle is in the category of "least concern."

The bald eagle lives across North America. At one time the bald eagle was in danger of going extinct. The eagle is now protected and its population is growing.

SAVE the ANIMALS!

ADOPT AN ANIMAL

Adopt an animal or give money to charities such as WWF. Adopting an animal is when you pay money each month to a charity. You get sent lots of information about the animal you have adopted and how your money is helping them.

Which grassland animal would you want to adopt?

SPREAD THE WORD!

Why not make a poster about an issue you learned about in this book, such as poaching, farming, or habitat loss?

Learn all you can about the subject and teach others about it too!

23

GLOSSARY

captivity	kept in a zoo or safari park and not in the wild
grazing	eating grass or similar plants throughout the day
habitat	the natural home in which animals, plants, and other living things live
illegally	to do something that is against the law
poaching	illegally hunting and killing an animal
polluted	when humans have made something dirty or harmful
population	the number of animals in a species
protected	looked after and kept safe
risk	when there is a chance that something might happen
species	a group of very similar animals or plants that can create young together
threatened	not sure of whether a type of animal or plant will survive

INDEX

Africa 10, 13, 16 17, 19
farming 5, 9, 12, 15, 17, 20, 23
habitats 5, 8 9, 12–15, 17, 20, 23

horns 10
humans 9, 13
hunting 10, 13–14, 16, 18
meat 14, 16, 18

North America 21
poaching 10–11, 16, 19, 23
roads 17
tusks 16